**SURVIVING TERROR**

# TRUE TEEN STORIES FROM AROUND THE WORLD

True Teen Stories from

# SOMALIA

## Surviving War and al-Shabaab

**Anna Maria Johnson**

Cavendish
Square

New York

Published in 2019 by Cavendish Square Publishing, LLC
243 5th Avenue, Suite 136, New York, NY 10016

Library of Congress Cataloging-in-Publication Data

Names: Johnson, Anna Maria, author.
Title: True teen stories from Somalia : surviving war and al-Shabaab / Anna
Maria Johnson.
Description: First edition. | New York : Cavendish Press, 2018. | Series:
Surviving terror : true teen stories from around the world | Grade level
7-12. | Includes bibliographical references and index.
Identifiers: LCCN 2018000185 (print) | LCCN 2018001383 (ebook) | ISBN
9781502635488 (eBook) | ISBN 9781502635471 (library
bound) | ISBN 9781502635495 (paperback)
Subjects: LCSH: Youth and war--Somalia. | Youth--Somalia--Social
conditions--21st century. | Somalia--Social conditions--21st century. |
Shabaab (Organization) | Terrorism--Somalia. | Child soldiers--Somalia.
Classification: LCC HQ799.2.W37 (ebook) | LCC HQ799.2.W37
J64 2018 (print) | DDC 303.660835096773--dc23
LC record available at https://lccn.loc.gov/2018000185

Editorial Director: David McNamara
Editor: Caitlyn Miller
Copy Editor: Rebecca Rohan
Associate Art Director: Amy Greenan
Designer: Christina Shults
Production Assistant: Karol Szymczuk

The photographs in this book are used by permission and through the courtesy of:
Cover Abdulfitah Hashi Nor/AFP/Getty Images; p. 4 John Cantlie/Getty Images; p. 7 Rainer Lesniewski/
Shutterstock.com; p. 15 Robert Harding/Alamy Stock Photo; p. 18 US Federal Government/Wikimedia
Commons/File:ACSS LOGO edited.jpg/Public Domain; p. 24 George Philipas/Alamy Stock Photo; p.
33 AFP Photo/Au-Un Ist Photo/Tobin Jones/Getty Images; p. 42 Nour Gelle Gedi/Anadolu Agency/
Getty Images; p. 44 Mohamed Sheikh Nor/AP Images; p. 47 Farah Abdi Warsameh/AP Images; p. 50
Washington County Jail/AP Images; p. 62, 86 Mohamed Abdiwahab/AFP/Getty Images; p. 65 Feisal
Omar/Reuters/Newscom; p. 75, 77 Free Wind 2014/Shutterstock.com; p. 80 Stu Forster/Getty Images;
p. 84 Khaled Fazaa/AFP/Getty Images; p. 89 Kenyan Presidential Press Service/Getty Images.

Printed in the United States of America

# CONTENTS

Teens from Afgooye, a town controlled by the terrorist group al-Shabaab, watch as foreign troops approach in February 2012.

# CHAPTER ONE

# SOMALIA AND AL-SHABAAB

When Bilan was just fourteen years old, she was kidnapped by members of a terrorist group called al-Shabaab outside Somalia's capital city of Mogadishu. Her father pleaded for her release but was told the entire family would be killed if he continued to protest. Bilan was forced to marry an al-Shabaab fighter and contribute to their cause. A year later, Bilan was released to return to her family—along with the baby born to her during her captivity.

When Mohamed was fifteen, he joined al-Shabaab and was put in change of twenty children his own age and younger. Soon afterward, he was badly injured in fighting against the Somali National Armed Forces. These are just two Somali teens out of the many thousands whose lives have been disrupted by al-Shabaab. Yet in the face of terrible violence, the people of Somalia—especially young people—continue to work toward building a peaceful and prosperous nation. Though the obstacles are numerous, they demonstrate that there is hope after terror strikes.

# Understanding Somalia

## Geography

Somalia, which means "Land of the Somali People," forms the eastern edge of the Horn of Africa. This coastal nation separates Ethiopia from the Indian Ocean on the east and from the Gulf of Aden in the north. North of the water lies Yemen, part of the Middle East, which in recent years has hosted large numbers of Somali refugees for reasons that will be explained in this book. The southern part of Somalia borders Kenya, and the northwest part of Somalia, now called Somaliland, borders Djibouti. Djibouti was previously part of Somalia but was colonized by the French and later given its independence.

Somaliland, a region that was once a British colony, declared itself independent from the rest of Somalia (formerly an Italian colony) in 1991, at the start of the Somali civil war, but the international community does not officially recognize its status. Humanitarian organizations group categorize Somaliland under the same heading of "Somalia" for convenience but acknowledge its different structure of governance. Recently, the government of Somalia has been in talks with Somaliland to discuss their

Somaliland (shown with green diagonal lines) declared its independence from the rest of Somalia (yellow) in 1991, but the international community groups them together. Across the border lie Ethiopia and Kenya (both in gray).

relationship. As the new government of Somalia gains strength, there is a possibility the two will reunite.

In between Somaliland to the northwest and the main body of Somalia in the south lies another special region called Puntland, which has been semiautonomous since 1998. This means the region considers itself as distinct from the rest of Somalia but has not sought independence. Again, humanitarian organizations and the international community group Puntland together with Somaliland and Somalia. The World Health Organization (WHO) carefully notes the differences between what it refers to as the three "zones" of Somalia: northwestern (Somaliland); northeastern (Puntland); and southern Somalia. Somaliland and Puntland each have their own judicial, legislative, and executive systems separate from the Somali government.

President Hassan Sheikh Mohamud was elected by clan leaders in September 2012, marking a significant transition from over two decades of civil war to a new federal government. Then in February 2017, a Somali American named Mohamed Abdullahi Mohamed was elected as the new president. He has expressed a strong commitment to end the power of al-Shabaab.

## Population and Daily Life

Somalia is special because it is among the oldest of homelands for human beings. Cave paintings found in Laas Geel, Somaliland, are estimated to date back to at least five thousand years ago. Interestingly, the country today includes different groups of people that live according to different patterns of survival. It includes pastoralists (nomadic herders), agrarians (growers of crops, primarily at a subsistence level), and modern urbanites who live in cities with lifestyles similar to that of people in other urban areas around the world.

# AN AL-SHABAAB LEADER WHO TURNED HIMSELF IN

According to the Middle Eastern news network Al Jazeera, Sheikh Mukhtar Robow was one of the founders of al-Shabaab—and the only founder who still survives. He, along with fighters who were loyal to him, defected from al-Shabaab in 2013 because of disagreements with others in its leadership. After living for a few years in the jungle while fighting his former allies in al-Shabaab, he and his fighters finally surrendered to the Somali government in August 2017. His surrender came after he lost at least nineteen of his fighters to al-Shabaab. It was also after the United States canceled a $5 million reward that had been offered for his capture. It took the Somali government months of talks with this man before he finally turned himself in. They believe canceling the bounty was helpful in convincing Robow to surrender.

Robow was one of the founders of al-Shabaab's predecessor in 2001. He had studied in Sudan in the late 1990s, traveled to Afghanistan, and trained alongside al-Qaeda, another global terrorist group, in 2000. From 2001 to 2013, according to the US government, he served as an "al-Shabaab spokesman, military commander and spiritual leader who planned and executed deadly attacks on Somali government troops and African Union peacekeeping forces."

This rich diversity poses difficulties as well, as different clans struggle to maintain their traditional values and ways of life in a land that is prone to intermittent droughts and severe lack of resources such as water and food. For example, clans that survive by growing their own crops sometimes resent others that survive by migration. This is because the animals of migrating groups sometimes devour crops as they pass through the landscape. On the other hand, pastoralists can resent agrarians who disrupt traditional migration patterns and restrict access to water. Meanwhile, in urban areas like Mogadishu, people hold jobs familiar to modern societies.

About 70 percent of the population lives in southern and central Somalia. Since there has not been an accurate census since the 1970s, no one knows for sure how many people live in the country. However, the WHO estimated the total population of all three zones at about 10.8 million people as of 2015. Human Rights Watch provides a figure of 12.3 million people (April 2017). The CIA's *World Factbook* estimates just over 11 million as of July 2017. Most sources agree that of the total population, half or more needs humanitarian assistance in order to meet basic needs like food and water.

The country as a whole has very low rates of formal education and employment, resulting in poor economic outcomes. The WHO reported in 2014 that only 20 percent of Somalian children attended primary school, which was arguably the lowest rate of any African country. It's estimated that about 80 percent of the people are illiterate. The low rate of literacy is in part because an entire generation of Somalis grew up under civil war, when educational facilities were completely destroyed.

Nonetheless, the Somali people have a rich oral tradition of storytelling and poetry. YouTube hosts videos of Somali poets, rappers, and musicians who keep alive their oral traditions. One British Somali poet born in Kenya, named Warsan Shire, became well known when Beyoncé quoted her poetry in the visual album *Lemonade*. Other Somali cultural activities include traditional dancing and singing, and sports including soccer and basketball, but these activities have all been forbidden in areas controlled by al-Shabaab.

Overall, most Somali people are young. The CIA *World Factbook* reports a median age of just eighteen years, meaning that half of the people are children or teenagers. Other sources estimate an even younger median age, perhaps around sixteen. Just 4 percent of the population is older than fifty-five years. By comparison, the median age in the United States is thirty-eight years, and about 28 percent of Americans are fifty-five or older. In Canada, the median age is forty-two years, and about one-third of Canadians are age fifty-five or older.

The reason why Somalia has such a young population, unfortunately, is because of civil war and instability. In addition, problems like food and water shortages due to frequent droughts, and lack of access to basic medical care, lead to a situation where the majority of people die before they reach old age. Only a few other countries in the world have such young populations. Among them are Uganda, Niger, Angola, Central African Republic, Democratic Republic of Congo, and the Gaza Strip—all of which are also regions experiencing severe levels of conflict.

Despite Somalia's undeniable problems such as war, famine, drought, extremism, and lack of strong governance, the Somali people are independent, resilient, and proud of their heritage. They place high value on their customs, their faith, their kin, and their vibrant oral tradition. Most of the people in Somalia are ethnically Somali, although about 15 percent are Bantu or Arab in descent. People of Somali ethnic descent also live in the Ogaden of Ethiopia and in the North Eastern Province of Kenya. This means the physical boundaries of these countries don't match the cultural and ethnic boundaries, creating ongoing tension.

## Religion

Virtually all Somali people follow the religion of Islam and have done so since the seventh century CE. Historically, the Somali people adhere to a large branch of Islam called Sunni. Sunnism is fairly tolerant of other branches of Islam and of other faiths and is influenced by Sufi beliefs. (Sufism is considered the more mystical branch of Islam.) Another branch of Islam, called Wahhabi (or Salafist ideology), has taken root in Eastern Africa since the 1980s. It is stricter, forbidding music and sports, and includes harsh punishments like amputating limbs for stealing or stoning women accused of adultery. The Wahhabi type of Islamic law, called sharia law, is prevalent in the Middle Eastern Gulf States and is promoted by radical groups like al-Shabaab. Al-Shabaab is heavily influenced by this Salafist ideology, which is intolerant not only of non-Muslims, but also of moderate Muslims.

Religion affects many aspects of daily life, including fashion. Women in Somalia wear colorful, beautiful fabrics that cover the body modestly but are not strictly prescribed. Women's clothing represents a combination of fashion and modesty. In the past, and in some regions today, women could wear more modern or Western-style clothing, such as athletic wear for playing sports or swimwear for competitive swimming. More recently, however, women in many parts of Somalia have become more restricted in how they are permitted to dress in public. Strict rules enforced by al-Shabaab mandate that women cover their hair with a scarf and wear specific types of clothing. Some of the different types of garments for women and girls are the hijab, the burka, the jilbab, and the niqab. Women who defy the dress code are sometimes harassed, physically harmed, or even killed.

Men also have certain dress requirements for modesty, including wearing long sleeves and long pants. Conservative men sometimes wear a type of linen tunic called a qamis and are forbidden to shave their beards.

## Clan Structure

More than in most countries today, Somalia is organized, sustained, and governed by clan structures rather than by a strong federal government. Clan leaders help to stabilize the society, make decisions, and resolve disputes. Leaders use customary, or traditional, law (also called *Xeer*) in combination with Islamic law to work out disagreements within and between clans. The major clans are the Hawiye, Isaaq, Daarood, Rahanwayn, Dir, and Digil. In the early days of Somalia's independence, an effort was made to downplay the role of clans and focus instead on a unified national government. But events of the 1980s and 1990s weakened support for the national government and made possible the rise of clan politics and clan warlords, which played a role in the destabilizing and eventual collapse of the Somali government in the early 1990s. In the absence of a central

Women in Berbera, Somaliland, wear the traditional, colorful jilbab over the top of other traditional or Western-style clothing.

government, clans provided governance and structure for Somali society.

## Origins of Al-Shabaab

Around 1999, an organization of several Islamist groups called the Islamic Courts Union (ICU) attempted to restore order and stability to the fractured state. The ICU remained influential throughout Somalia during the early 2000s. They believed that the way to bring order was to implement sharia law, a strict form of Islam, which forbids activities such as listening to popular music and playing sports. Even though most Somali people were ready for an end to violent civil war, they did not all welcome the stringent new rules nor the violent and coercive methods used to implement them. Women, in particular, faced strict new requirements about what they could wear. For example, the niqab, a veil that reveals only the woman's eyes, became required in regions where the ICU took over. In 2006, the ICU captured

Mogadishu and other territories, prompting interventions by Ethiopia and the African Union. Defeated, the ICU splintered apart. But extremism didn't go away.

A radical offshoot of this group grew into what is today known as al-Shabaab, which means "the youth," because it was largely composed of young people with radical, extremist ideas. In Western news sources, al-Shabaab is sometimes spelled variously as Al-Shabaab (with a capital A), Al-Shabab or simply The Shabaab ("al" means "the" in Arabic). Al-Shabaab opposed the unified transitional federal government that had been put into place in 2004 with international support. They also opposed international interventions from Ethiopia, the United States, the African Union, and the United Nations. Although many different opinions exist within the group, much of its leadership has the goal of creating a unified Greater Somalia that would include the Somali parts of neighboring countries (Ogaden in Ethiopia and the North Eastern Province in Kenya). Al-Shabaab leadership wants Somalia to be ruled under a strict form of Islamic (sharia) law— stricter than even the rules of the ICU.

In 2009, al-Shabaab emerged as a powerful actor in the region. It gained strength over the next few years through terrorizing large areas of the country, recruiting child soldiers, and preventing humanitarian aid from reaching people in need of food and medicine. In 2011, their actions destroyed crops and infrastructure to the point that famine killed about 260,000 people and many more suffered malnutrition and stunted growth. Al-Shabaab's strength peaked in 2013, then began to diminish as other powerful groups committed to fighting them. As of November 2017, they still control about 20 percent (one-fifth) of the land area of Somalia. It's believed that about seven thousand to nine thousand fighters were still active in 2017. While they are no longer as powerful and organized as they once were, they continue to carry out attacks within Somalia and outside the country, including in Kenya.

Many have wondered how what began as a small band of radicals became such a powerful and terrible force in Eastern Africa. People have asked where they got enough funding to gain influence and power. Others have wanted to understand how a group that promotes violence and terror manages to persuade others to join them. While experts have had difficulty studying the region due to instability, some of the answers can be explored.

## Funding

Al-Shabaab's funding comes from a variety of sources, including donations from the Somali diaspora (Somali people living in other countries), other governments, charitable

# THE AFRICA CENTER FOR STRATEGIC STUDIES

The Africa Center for Strategic Studies, located at the National Defense University in Washington, DC, originated in the 1990s after bipartisan conversations within the US House of Representatives' National Security Committee. According to their website, in response to the National Security Committee's request, the US Department of Defense created a center to "encourage a broader understanding on the African continent of military matters compatible with democratic principles and civilian control." The center provides education and research related to topics like "regional security, conflict management, health and security, energy and security, and counterterrorism." The Africa Center approach includes military and police but also civilian, legislative, and civil society security actors.

The Africa Center for Strategic Studies was founded in 1999.

The Africa Center has held more than 150 programs, involving fifteen thousand participants. It also engages Washington policymakers to help improve Africa security issues. In 2009, the Africa Center established a research section to provide better information for both African and US policymakers.

organizations, and taxes collected by al-Shabaab members from local people.

Funding also has come partly from piracy, as desperate young Somali men have used boats to attack international shipping routes, taking supplies, weapons, and other goods. Piracy decimated the Gulf of Aden in the early 2000s. It is worth noting that the problem of piracy has its own complicated origins and is only tangentially related to al-Shabaab. Although piracy has largely diminished in the region, a few attacks occasionally occur, including at least one reported in 2017.

By land, members of al-Shabaab raid towns and villages as well as shipping ports. Fighters hold people at gunpoint and demand whatever money and resources they have.

## Recruitment

Both voluntary and forced recruitment have been carried out with a variety of strategies and means. Recruits include both males and females. Some are recruited for pay, while others are not.

In order to recruit more soldiers to their cause, al-Shabaab has used a variety of approaches including posting videos and appeals over social media and other internet platforms. Overall, however, since the internet has very limited reach in this country, most recruiting efforts take place in person at the local level.

Within Somalia, al-Shabaab leadership sometimes promises money and food for the families of young men who agree to join the fight. Other tactics are more coercive and violent. At times, groups of al-Shabaab fighters have raided schools, using heavy weapons to threaten children and teens if they did not join. Boys have been taken as fighters, and girls have been abducted as wives against their will.

## Responding to al-Shabaab

The global community took notice as more and more Somali people fled their country to seek refuge in the Middle East, Europe, and North America. In 2007, neighboring Ethiopia sent fighters to put down the instability in the region and attempt to restore a federal government to the fractured nation of Somalia. The African Union, an organization similar to the United Nations but consisting entirely of African nations, also organized troops from Uganda and other African countries, known as AMISOM, to assist with putting down al-Shabaab. The United States joined the fray too.

In 2017, multiple militaries are present and active in Somalia including the Somali national military, AMISOM

(African Union troops), Ethiopian military, the US troops, various clan militia groups, and, of course, al-Shabaab.

Military intervention is not the only strategy used to fight al-Shabaab. Humanitarian aid groups use nonviolent means to combat the group by providing education, medical care, food, and psychosocial counseling. All strategies aim to give vulnerable people better options than fighting for al-Shabaab. Recent research suggests that "soft methods" such as offering aid, improving infrastructure, improving the rule of law, and improving the political process may be more effective than the military strikes.

## Consequences for Somalis

It is difficult to describe all the ways in which al-Shabaab and the previous two decades of civil strife have affected the Somali people. One method is to look at the numbers. There are more than one million internally displaced people (IDP). This describes people who have been forced to leave their homes due to violence but have not left the country to immigrate elsewhere. The United Nations Refugee Agency (UNHCR) estimated in December 2016 that there were more than 1.5 million IDP. By the summer of 2017, this estimate had risen to 1.7 million. More than two-thirds of these displaced people are under eighteen years of age.

A combination of drought and flooding in 2016 and 2017 resulted in severe food shortages. These shortages led to further internal displacement, but al-Shabaab's terrorist activities limited access to humanitarian aid and medical care in emergencies. For instance, food brought in by outside agencies was sometimes stolen by al-Shabaab and withheld from those who needed it. Furthermore, some humanitarian workers have been killed. Even journalists trying to report on the drought and conflicts have been jailed or killed by al-Shabaab.

Within Somalia's borders, those who remain struggle because the infrastructure is underdeveloped. Only 2 percent of the population has internet access, which is among the lowest rates worldwide. Roads are often damaged or blocked by al-Shabaab or other armed groups, especially in the southern part of the country where al-Shabaab has more power.

In addition to the Somali people displaced within their country's borders, additional numbers have left the country as refugees seeking safety, food, and health care elsewhere. The UNHCR reported in 2016 a high number of Somali refugees living in Kenya (313,255), Yemen (256,169), Ethiopia (249,903), Uganda (35,373), Djibouti (13,077), and Eritrea (2,246). There are additional refugees in other countries.

## Mulki Haji Hassan's Story

UNICEF's website provided a platform for one fifteen-year-old Somali girl to share her story. Mulki Haji Hassan traveled north to the relative safety of Puntland, where she and her family live in a temporary camp:

> We left our home in Mogadishu and came to Galkayo because of the war. But there was fighting there. Last year, my little brother was killed in an explosion so we moved to this camp. I can't walk—I was born with a bone disease. I'd like to have my legs straightened but we cannot afford it ... We eat rice, but sometimes we go hungry. They brought food here once but now it's gone and we have nothing ... I have nine brothers and sisters but we don't have any schools. In the future I want to study and become a teacher.

Hassan's story shows how the effects of terrorism and war can ripple outward, affecting every facet of life from food to education to health care.

The Mosque of Islamic Solidarity in Mogadishu overlooks the Indian Ocean.
It was built in 1987 and is the main mosque in Somalia's capital city.

# CHAPTER TWO

# THE RISE OF AL-SHABAAB

As a result of historical events and other complexities within Somali culture, the country has been described as among the most dangerous nations in which to be a woman. The Africa Center for Strategic Studies called al-Shabaab the deadliest Islamist extremist group in Africa in 2016 because it was responsible for the deaths of more than 4,200 people. Many factors have contributed to the current fragile situation, making life difficult for teenagers and their families in Somalia today.

# An Overview of Somalia's History

Islam arrived in Somalia as long ago as the seventh century and has remained an important influence over Somali culture and government ever since. Throughout the seventh to the nineteenth centuries, the country was ruled by a series of sultanates. Historians describe it as a once-powerful empire.

## Colonialism

In the nineteenth century, thanks to the Suez Canal, European colonialism reached the eastern coast of Africa. In the 1860s, France became involved with an area of the Somali coast that eventually would become the country of Djibouti. Soon afterward, in 1887, Britain proclaimed itself protectorate over the northwestern region. Not to be outdone, Italy responded by setting up its own protectorate over much of Somalia in 1889, also including adjacent parts of what are today Zanzibar and Kenya.

In 1905, Italy purchased the city of Mogadishu, adorning it with Roman-style architecture that graced the capital until twenty-first-century violence ruined much of it. In essence, the nineteenth century saw two colonial "Somalilands," a British protectorate to the northwest and an Italian colony to the northeast and south. During the 1930s, Somali-speaking parts of Ethiopia were added to Italian Somaliland to form Italian East Africa.

In the early 1940s, the Italians occupied British Somaliland, then the British occupied Italian Somaliland. Eventually, in 1960, both colonies gained their independence and joined into one country called the United Republic of Somalia.

## From Democracy to Dictatorship

Not quite a decade into its independence, in 1969, the third elected president of Somalia, Abdirashid Ali Shermarke, was assassinated in a coup. Mohamed Siad Barre declared himself the new president and declared Somalia a socialist state. This began a two-decade dictatorship. On one hand, the dictatorship brought Somalia modern developments such as infrastructure, a public education system, a written language, and better economic and educational opportunities for women. On the other hand, the Barre regime did not always respect human rights for individuals, and anyone who criticized the government could be cruelly treated. During the later years of Barre's regime, he played clans against one another to cement his own power. The divisions Barre created persist to this day.

In the mid-1970s, widespread drought in the Horn of Africa led to starvation as the strictly government-run economy failed to provide adequate food for the Somali people. Around this same time, an underground movement formed in response to the Barre regime. Barre had envisioned a secular (nonreligious), socialist state. He took harsh tactics to try to make that happen. Because his secular tactics failed, dissenters imagined that an extremist Islamist approach might be better. In 1983, a secret Somali Islamist group formed. It was composed of Somalis who had studied in Egypt and Saudi Arabia, where they had been influenced by the Muslim Brotherhood, the oldest political Islamist group in the Arab world. This secret Somali group was nicknamed AIAI or Islamic Unity. It began doing important humanitarian and social support work in the southern and central parts of Somalia. As a result, it built goodwill and gained support from the local people. Their goal was to remove Barre, along with his socialism, and to create a Greater Somalia state that would unite all Somalis in the Horn of Africa (including those in Ethiopia, Djibouti, and Kenya). Many of their ideals and charitable works were good, but some members of this group supported the use of violence and had little tolerance for people with different viewpoints than their own.

## Border Disputes Between Somalia and Its Neighbors

During the 1960s, Somalia was entangled in border disputes with two of its neighbors, Kenya and Ethiopia. These disputes were caused in part by the fact that Somali-speaking people lived there, and Somalia wanted to include these populations within its borders. The origins of these border disputes go back centuries. As one example, during the nineteenth century, the British gave grazing lands (which contained Somali people) in a region called Ogaden over to Ethiopian Emperor Menelik. This land has been the subject of many subsequent clashes between Ethiopia and Somalia.

Expert Jakkie Cilliers wrote an article titled "Violent Islamist Extremism and Terror in Africa," which discusses how the desire for all the Somali people to be united in one Greater Somalia (with an Islamic identity) has combined with the failure to resolve the status of Somalis living outside their nation's border. Cilliers states these factors led to the rise of al-Shabaab. Cilliers and other experts name other key factors as well. These include the brutality of the Barre regime in the 1970s and 1980s, the importation of a more stringent view of Islam (Salafism) from other Middle Eastern countries, and the lack of resolution of colonial era disputes, among others.

Other experts have identified additional drivers including economic impoverishment, inequality among clans, marginalization of certain groups, and low levels of education.

The relationship between Somalia and Ethiopia, as mentioned above, has often been fraught with tension over borders and power arrangements. In July 1977, Barre led Somalia to invade the Ogaden. But in the dispute, the Soviet Union sided with Ethiopia. Along with some help from Cuban and South Yemeni brigades, they pushed Barre out of the Ogaden.

When the Soviet Union became involved in the Horn of Africa, the United States, in a somewhat surprising alliance, supported the Barre regime, even though he led a socialist state and the United States aimed to promote democracy.

## Fragmentation

Amidst all the commotion, civil war erupted in Somalia. The Barre regime collapsed in 1991 amid widespread clan-based conflicts. President Barre's military regime was overthrown, resulting in anarchy and instability as the region collapsed into chaos. Rival warlords divided the country into fiefdoms without a central authority, each doing as he saw fit. Amidst all this conflict, the AIAI (Islamic Unity) emerged as a viable power in the region. It received funding from Somalis who had fled the country and resettled elsewhere (the Somali diaspora) and by wealthy Saudis, including Osama bin Laden. The AIAI would later team up with a group of sharia courts known as the Islamic Courts Union (ICU). Because the AIAI served as the youth militia of the ICU, it later earned the name al-Shabaab.

Meanwhile, in 1991, the former British colony Somaliland, in the northwest, became disgusted with the chaos in the rest of the country. Somaliland declared itself independent and set up its own executive, judiciary, and legislative systems. They continue to function, more or less, until this day. As a result, Somaliland has not suffered under terrorism and civil war to the same degree as the rest of Somalia.

During the early 1990s, the United States continued to be involved in Somalia, leading a United Nations–backed peacekeeping mission. In 1993, eighteen US troops were killed during the Battle of Mogadishu, in an incident nicknamed "Black Hawk Down." By 1995, the peacekeeping mission had failed entirely. The United States stepped out of Somalia and did not get involved again for several years.

In 1998, having seen Somaliland's independence, the northern region of Puntland declared itself autonomous. Puntland did not go so far as to declare its independence. However, it did set up its own judiciary, legislative, and

# AL-SHABAAB VERSUS WOMEN'S BASKETBALL

Teens living in Somalia face extraordinary limitations on activities like playing sports and listening to music because of al-Shabaab and religious extremism. Women's basketball player Aisha, of Mogadishu, told her story to a writer for the *New Yorker* magazine. At age fourteen, Aisha began receiving threatening phone calls from men who told her that Islam doesn't allow women to play sports or to wear pants. Over the phone, they threatened to kill her if she didn't quit basketball. Her mother, Warsan, had played basketball as a youth when extremists did not have as much influence. But Warsan feared for her daughter because Warsan knew that members of al-Shabaab really had been known to kill people for playing or even watching sports on television. Aisha's former teammate Amaal had a friend named Faiza who was abducted, tortured, and killed for playing the game. Aisha was afraid when she heard about this. However, she stuck with it because basketball was everything to her, and she was an independent-minded young woman. She is a devout Muslim but doesn't believe that Allah forbids women from playing sports.

Once when Aisha and two of her friends called a taxi to transport them home after a practice, the driver pulled over and made a phone call. Another man appeared with a gun, calling them "infidels" because they had been playing sports and wearing pants. He fired at one of the girls, and the bullet grazed her leg. When the girls contacted the police, the man was arrested.

"I go beyond everything just to get to the court," says Aisha. Aisha's friend Amaal agrees, "To have a dream and wear pants and a shirt and hold a basketball—there's nothing stronger to me. To think about what I want for myself and to do it."

Somalian teens, both boys and girls, enjoy a basketball training session in Mogadishu, in 2013.

executive systems. While Puntland has since suffered from piracy and some terrorist activities to a greater degree than Somaliland, it has been spared the level of violence and discord that virtually decimated the south-central zone. In both Somaliland and Puntland, the governing structures have taken into account the strong role of clans, allowing clan leaders to express their voices in decision-making and relying on traditional (customary) law to resolve disputes.

Finally, after almost two decades of ongoing civil war, in 2000, a new unity government formed with international backing. Clan leaders elected a new president, but this attempted government never gained strength. By 2001, Ethiopia supported some Somali warlords who didn't want to follow the new administration. The situation deteriorated. Then Somalia was visited by natural disaster in 2004 when a tsunami displaced thousands of people on the Somali coast.

By this time, the Somali people were suffering under the effects of more than a decade of civil war. The education and health care systems had completely collapsed, resulting in widespread illiteracy and rising rates of maternal and infant mortality. In addition, agriculture had been hit hard by intermittent droughts. Those droughts meant that more than half the country's population had to rely on humanitarian aid for their most basic needs. Water, food, and medicine needed to be provided by aid groups. In such desperate circumstances, diseases festered. Malaria, tuberculosis, leprosy, and many other illnesses spread rapidly. Many could have easily been prevented by vaccines—if only the infrastructure and organization were there to provide them.

Humanitarian organizations such as the World Health Organization and UNICEF, nongovernmental organizations (NGOs), and many others did their best to dispense food, clean water, hygiene supplies, and medicine to the people who needed it. But violence and the lack of telecommunications made every effort unimaginably difficult. The World Health Organization reported in 2004 that the situation in Somalia was as unstable as at any time previous and raised alarm about escalating health risks.

Into these circumstances and this power vacuum swept various militia groups, including AIAI (which later became al-Shabaab) and the ICU. In the absence of a properly functioning educational system, humanitarian aid groups set up schools and other educational facilities. Some of these charities, however, were funded by ideologically minded groups. Two examples are the Saudi-funded al-Haramain Islamic Foundation and the Revival of Islamic Heritage Society, a Kuwaiti NGO. Both of these charities also had financial links to al-Qaeda, which is today recognized as a terrorist organization. Many of the schools, or madrasas, which these groups funded included a rigid view of Islam.

Many peace activists today blame the ideological teaching of these madrasas for promoting extremist views, in contrast to the more moderate views of Islam traditionally held in Somalia.

In June 2006, the ICU and AIAI (al-Shabaab) seized the capital of Mogadishu and much of the southern part of the country, defeating the US-backed Alliance for the Restoration of Peace and Counter-Terrorism, which had been set up in 2004. Hundreds of people were injured or killed in violence between the militias and clan warlords.

Ethiopia, motivated by renewed worries over the Ogaden as well as the general instability of the region, intervened in its neighbor's troubles in December 2006. African Union forces known as AMISOM followed up, especially from 2007 to 2011. These African Union forces were sent by other African nations with the intention of restoring order and peace, but many Somalis viewed them—and the Ethiopian troops—as an invading threat. As of late 2017, about 24,000 AMISOM troops remain in Somalia to help reinforce the Somali National Army and the developing federal government.

## Modern-day Pirates

As if all this conflict were not enough, from 2005–2012, Somali pirates plagued the seas, posing problems for international trade. The Gulf of Aden, at that time, was the most dangerous shipping route in the world. It started with local Somali fishermen whose livelihoods were being threatened by illegal fishing by foreigners. An informal group of young men banded together to resist illegal fishing vessels and were given money by the foreign fishermen if they agreed to go away. Before long, what began as the well-intentioned defense of Somali fishing grounds devolved into a lucrative piracy practice. By 2008, the level of piracy was severe enough that the UN Security Council allowed foreign countries to send war ships to battle the Somali pirates, which took years and multipronged strategic approaches to get under control. Had Somalia had a functioning, powerful government to protect its fishing grounds, none of this would have happened.

Despite all the difficulties of 2006, by the end of the year, airports and seaports were reopened for the first time since 1995. Peace talks began in Khartoum, Sudan. But also around that same time, Somalia had its first known suicide bombing. The international community helped to create a transitional government which, along with backing from the Ethiopian government, worked together to take back Mogadishu. Meanwhile, sometime in 2007, the United States returned to action and initiated air strikes against al-Qaeda in southern Somalia. As the transitional government gained international support, resistance by al-Shabaab gained strength.

## A Downward Spiral into Famine and Terror

As described above, the Islamic Courts (ICU) had used violence in 2006 to take Mogadishu and other parts of southern Somalia from clan warlords. Ethiopian and transitional government representatives began peace talks with the ICU. By January 2007, the ICU fighters had abandoned their strongholds. Some members of the Islamist groups did not want to see this happen, however, so they broke away into the extremist group today known as al-Shabaab. The fighting continued and rages on to this day.

In 2009, al-Shabaab captured the highly populated city of Baidoa, then moved to Mogadishu and advanced south, taking over large swaths of territory. The transitional government of Somalia was powerless to stop them. Al-Shabaab became feared as they took extreme measures to secure their power. For example, in 2010, CNN reported that militants publicly executed two teenage girls, ages fifteen and sixteen, for being "spies for the government." The girls were told to stand in front of a tree and were shot. A relative of one of the girls said, "Ayan didn't have any contact with the government and even in her life, she never had a mobile [phone] so we can't understand how she could be accused of being a spy." A third teenage girl had been stoned to death in 2009 by al-Shabaab.

One of the worst periods of modern Somali history came in late 2010–2011, when another famine hit the region. Although droughts are a regular feature of life in the Horn of Africa, it was human action that transformed this drought into a famine. Under a well-managed government and social structure, food can be imported and distributed fairly to meet the needs of people living in drought conditions. But in the absence of a functioning state, the problem escalated to dire levels.

During this disaster, al-Shabaab prevented some of the international food aid from reaching people, and an estimated 260,000 people died of starvation. In addition, children and others suffered malnourishment to an extent that impacted not only the health of individuals, but Somali social structure for decades to come. This is because malnourishment in children can not only stunt their growth but also permanently damage their cognition and thinking skills. A generation of children was cheated of the opportunity to reach their full potential.

In 2012, al-Shabaab announced a merger with al-Qaeda, the terrorist organization responsible for plotting the attacks on New York's World Trade Center and the Pentagon in Washington, DC, on September 11, 2001. The merger was controversial within al-Shabaab's leadership because some of its members wanted to keep their focus on their homeland (Somalia) while others wanted to connect with other Islamist extremists across North Africa and the Middle East. Divisions within the leadership would eventually weaken al-Shabaab.

Yet al-Shabaab continued to recruit soldiers. Human Rights Watch reported in 2012 that al-Shabaab was targeting teens and children as young as ten to fight on the front lines. Teen girls were abducted to serve and forced to marry al-Shabaab fighters. One sixteen-year-old girl who refused to marry a much older commander was killed and beheaded. Her head was brought to her school to warn others to cooperate. A nineteen-year-old student reported on another girl his age who was shot at school in front of classmates because she refused to go with al-Shabaab.

## The Slow Journey toward Democracy and Peace

On the positive side, in 2012, a new Somali government was established. For the first time in more than twenty years, a formal parliament was sworn in. Although it was not a one-person, one-vote election (only clan leaders voted), it did represent the first presidential election since 1967! Somalia's government is based on strong clan representation, which was arranged out of necessity to prevent clan militias from rising up against the national leadership. Because clan leadership has historically been so vital in the region, any

# WOMEN'S BASKETBALL MAKES A COMEBACK

Since al-Shabaab has been ousted from many regions in Somalia, community sports are making a comeback. Kismayo, on Somalia's southern coast, was once home to a famous women's basketball team in the 1980s. After decades of civil war, followed by five years under al-Shabaab, sports had fallen by the wayside. According to US Aid's website, "participation in sports for young girls was even punishable by death under al-Shabaab." But now, the community is rebuilding. Girls are again learning to play the sport.The nation hosted a national tournament in 2017 in Garowe, Puntland, which was followed on Twitter by hundreds of thousands of Somalis. The last time the Somali Women's team had played outside the country was in 2011, when it played in the Pan Arab Games in Qatar. They'd placed fourth out of twenty-two countries. Prior to that game, they'd not played competitively since the civil war began in 1991.

In addition to al-Shabaab discouraging sports, some influential Muslim clerics known as the Somali Religious Council formally banned women's basketball in late December of 2016. But as basketball player Sahra Mohamud told the news organization VOA Somalia, "I play wearing my hijab on, and this is my favorite sport and I have a right to play as long as I am not against the major values and pillars of my religion. We see sport as a peace-building tool to bring the Somali people together."

Somalian fishermen with their boats near the capital city of Mogadishu in 2014. Fishing is an important part of Somalia's economy.

successful government must recognize their importance and take great pains to ensure representation of all clans. While other democracies may criticize how much influence clan leaders have, the reality is that this has been a successful strategy in moving Somalia toward peace. In January 2013, the United States officially recognized the Somali government in Mogadishu, lending additional global credibility.

At its peak in 2013, al-Shabaab controlled large areas of Somalia—more than the national government—and by 2017, it still controlled about 20 percent of the country. Periodically, al-Shabaab organizes raids in Kenya and Uganda. Although the Somali national government in 2017 is stronger than it has been in many years, and al-Shabaab no longer holds official power in much of the country, many of its members and former members still distrust the central government.

There is no doubt that al-Shabaab is weakening slowly while the Somali government gains strength. But it would be premature to say that al-Shabaab has been defeated. They continue to fight guerrilla-style, setting bombs and using suicide bombers. In October 2017, their deadliest strike ever killed over four hundred in Mogadishu and injured hundreds more. This proves that even when al-Shabaab is driven out, it can still sow terror. Yet international governments and nongovernmental organizations agree that, on the whole, the situation in Somalia is improving.

Perhaps the strongest evidence of progress is the number of Somali refugees who have chosen to return to their homeland. No one claims that the situation is stable yet. But evidence suggests that resilient and committed Somali people are making strides in bringing security to their homeland. The UN Refugee Agency reported in September 2017 that since March 2015, a total of 38,289 people have arrived back to Somalia from Kenya and Yemen (including 32,429 Somalis, 5,559 Yemenis, and 343 people from other countries).

Besides military action, efforts like providing food aid, increasing economic prosperity, and developing infrastructure will help to create viable alternatives for people who might otherwise join extremist groups out of desperation.

This child soldier was not part of al-Shabaab, but was rather working for the Somali government to patrol the Mogadishu streets in 2009. The Somali government has since stopped recruiting children as soldiers.

# CHAPTER THREE

# TEEN RECRUITS

Somalia has about 6.49 million adolescents and youth, according to UNFPA Somalia. About half of the youth between ages fifteen to nineteen are able to read. About half of adolescents attend school. But about 66 percent of people ages fifteen to thirty-five have never completed any level of schooling. Of people from ages fifteen to thirty-five, only 18 percent have completed primary level education (elementary school). Just 3 percent have completed university or college. As you can imagine, opportunities for young people to find good-paying work are low. In fact, the youth unemployment rate in Somalia is among the worst worldwide, at 67 percent. This creates difficult situations of poverty and lack of opportunity. These dire circumstances can make illicit activities such as joining a radical group like al-Shabaab or engaging in piracy seem like viable economic opportunities.

# Reasons for Joining al-Shabaab

Expert analysts at the Global Center on Cooperative Security have identified two sets of factors to explain why people join radical extremist groups. The first set of drivers are called "push" factors—these are things like underdevelopment in their country or region, lack of access to education or employment, and the sense of being an outsider. These factors can cause an individual to feel dissatisfied with life enough to be attracted to, or "pushed" to, violent extremism.

The second set of drivers are "pull" factors—reasons why the organization is able to pull recruits into its circle. Al-Shabaab and other groups like it seem appealing to vulnerable people because of the charismatic leaders who organize them, their strategic messaging, offers of financial and other benefits, or social status that members feel when they join.

Throughout the Greater Horn of Africa, a number of push factors have been observed. These include rising inequality (extreme gaps between the wealthy and poor), high unemployment, limited infrastructure, demographic shifts,

Al-Shabaab fighters display weapons as they conduct military exercises in northern Mogadishu, Somalia.

long-term refugee crises, and environmental degradation. Another important point to address is the problem of corruption. Even though the international community rejoiced at the 2017 Presidential election in Somalia taking place peacefully, a Somali news portal called *Goobjoog* reported that votes were trading at $1.3 million each!

Meanwhile, about 80 percent of the livestock in Somalia died in 2017 due to severe drought conditions. It is understandable that people suffering tremendous loss and damage might feel anger and resentment toward the government. Some potential recruits think that violent extremism is one way to reach their social and political goals when they don't find other, more appropriate channels. From another viewpoint, the promise of money and goods looks appealing when families are experiencing severe hunger and financial stress.

Within Somalia in particular, divisions along clan lines mean that some individuals have access to greater power and resources due to their kinship connections. Others are marginalized, especially if they belong to a minority group like the Bantu or a less powerful clan. Global Center experts explain, "Politics, control over state institutions, and access to public goods continue to be contested on the basis of clan lines, and inter-clan competition and mistrust have hardened over the course of more than two decades of conflict."

## Young Recruits

Many Americans and others outside the country of Somalia might picture al-Shabaab as a group of soldiers in their twenties and thirties, or perhaps even older. But the truth is that many fighters in this terrorist organization are children and teenagers, many of whom were forced against their will to join. Al-Shabaab has forcibly recruited children as young as ten to serve as frontline soldiers—like human shields to protect the older, more experienced soldiers behind them. Children and teens, both boys and girls, have also been used as suicide bombers.

It is impossible to know how many of al-Shabaab's fighters are teens because the lack of birth certificates in

Somalia makes it hard to know anyone's age. But UNICEF, Human Rights Watch, the CIA, and Amnesty International have found abundant evidence that many of the soldiers are very young. UN officials were able to document that al-Shabaab used 1,091 children as soldiers during 2016. (To be fair, UN officials also documented the use of 169 children by the Somali National Army, 415 by clan militia groups, and 67 by Ahlu Sunna Wal-jamea, or ASWJ, a political, social, and militant group.)

Some experts estimate that the majority of al-Shabaab fighters are currently between the ages of nineteen and twenty-five. One strategy to recruit soldiers has been for al-Shabaab fighters to invade a school and force the students to join. In these cases, they use violence or threats to compel teens or children to join—some are as young as ten when pressed into service. The US Department of State reports that child recruits in Somalia are subjected to inadequate food, physical punishment, weapons training, and harsh treatment. Children are used to punish and even execute other children. Al-Shabaab also uses children as human shields, suicide bombers, and to carry ammunition, water, and food. Children's other tasks include removing the dead and injured. Sometimes they are forced to plant roadside bombs.

Abu Musab from al-Shabaab brushed aside complaints from Human Rights Watch in 2012 about their use of child soldiers. He argued that Islam considers the age of adulthood to be fifteen years old. Tirana Hassan of Human Rights Watch told CNN in 2012, "We're beginning to see more and more instances where children are essentially being used as cannon fodder."

One teenage boy, whose name was withheld for his protection, survived being recruited by al-Shabaab and was able to speak to Human Rights Watch about his experience. He said that he and his friends were invited to play football at a nearby field. But when they arrived, he and the other kids were gathered up and sent to training camps. At the training camps, recruits suffered abuse including rape, assault, and forced marriages. Recruits from the ages of fourteen to seventeen were taken to the front line where they were mowed down by gunfire.

According to a 2012 CNN article, one fifteen-year-old boy from Mogadishu told Human Rights Watch how he and all his classmates had been taken to join al-Shabaab in 2010. He said, "Out of all my classmates—about one hundred boys—only two of us escaped, the rest were killed. The children were cleaned off. The children all died and the bigger soldiers ran away."

UN officials documented a total of 1,381 children abducted in 2016: 857 by al-Shabaab, 373 by the Somali National Army, 125 by clan militia, 12 by the ASWJ, 7 by

AMISOM troops, and 7 by unknown elements. Notably, al-Shabaab's recruitment of children increased, while work has been done to prevent child recruitment into the Somali National Army.

In addition to recruiting boys to be soldiers, sometimes al-Shabaab forces young women or teen girls to be married off to soldiers. These young women are forced to cook for the soldiers, bear children, and sometimes fight. One such girl, Fatoumah, told her story to Andrew Harding, Africa correspondent for the BBC News. As a teenager, Fatoumah was kidnapped by al-Shabaab while coming home from school one day. She remembers,

> They tortured me, and starved me. Then they raped me. Eventually I had to submit—that was the only way I could save myself. The torture lasted for eight months. They did bad things to me. Then they made me marry an Emir—a commander—of the group. One of my three children is his. The other two are from a different fighter. My first husband died. Then I was made to marry another. They were merciless. I was with al-Shabaab for three years ... I served the fighters food and water. When they went to war I had to provide first aid. We went into battle with

*them and even fought alongside them. One day we were in a convoy going to fight and there was an ambush by AMISOM. When I got wounded in my side they abandoned me. I went to hide in the bush. Later some people found me and gave me traditional medicine to heal my wound, then they took me by camel to a safer area.*

But Fatoumah was tracked by al-Shabaab. She reported, "I was part of them—and they didn't want me to leave. Whoever tries to leave must be killed. So they sent several people to kill me, including someone with a suicide vest—he blew himself up when he met me. That's why I have this scar on my head." At the time that Fatoumah was interviewed, she was just twenty. She was already scarred, widowed multiple times, and a mother of three.

## Socioeconomic Reasons to Join

Not all recruits are forced violently into joining the organization, however. In some cases, al-Shabaab promises jobs to youth who need the money to help their families. As mentioned before, there is very low access to education, and an extremely high unemployment rate (67 percent) for youth from ages fifteen to twenty-four. Only 6 percent of these young people are attending secondary school or pursuing other educational opportunities. Therefore, the lack of money combined with nothing productive to do makes these populations very vulnerable to being recruited by al-Shabaab or being lured into piracy or human smuggling. An offer of money, food, and security for one's family can sound too good to pass up. Or in some cases, young people might be on their own, since violence, famine, and migration have disrupted many family structures.

Even Kenyan teenagers have been recruited to join al-Shabaab in Somalia. Africa News reported in August 2017 that five Kenyan teenagers were arrested while traveling to Somalia. Three of them admitted that they had been en route to joining al-Shabaab but had changed their minds along the way. Two others simply confirmed that, yes, they were on their way and planned to join the fighting. Isiolo County in Kenya has noted many missing teens and suspects that al-Shabaab has recruited them.

# Ideological or Religious Reasons for Joining

For some recruits, being invited to fight for their religion was enough to bring them on board with al-Shabaab. A former member of al-Shabaab who had joined at a young age said, "No one forced me to join al-Shabaab. They were telling everyone to come and fight for Islam. So I joined up." This man, named Mohammed, had become a tax collector for al-Shabaab in his town. He explained the details of the role to the BBC: "We collected money from trucks bringing goods from Mogadishu. We took six million dollars a month." He claims that even after government forces retook the area, he and others were still collecting large sums of money for al-Shabaab. But at some point, Mohammed became disturbed by those in al-Shabaab who committed atrocities. He said, "Al-Shabaab terrorized their own community—forcing people to give more money than they can afford. It was all about money—not religion. Then I heard the government was granting amnesties to people who leave, so I took advantage of that."

At the time of the news story, Mohammed was living in a walled compound. There, former al-Shabaab members were given the chance to develop new job skills and other training to help them reintegrate with their communities apart from al-Shabaab.

Another youth, Hanat, said he had joined al-Shabaab as a teenager because he was unemployed and bored. Once he joined, he regretted it. Yet his bosses would not let him leave. He described the terrible experience in 2010 of fighting in

Mogadishu without enough ammunition or training. "We were fighting a hide-and-seek war," he described to Andrew Harding of the BBC. One night, Hanat violated the ban on using his cell phone and called his brother. He learned that his own brother was fighting on the front line for the government side, against al-Shabaab. Hanat changed his mind about which side he should be on, escaped, and made his way to Baidoa, where government forces had control. He called a government official, who welcomed Hanat to the camp for rehabilitating former al-Shabaab fighters.

# The Role of Technology in Recruitment

Most of al-Shabaab's fighters have been recruited in old-fashioned ways, face-to-face from within Somalia. But with new developments in technology, al-Shabaab has also been able to capitalize on social media such as Facebook, Instagram, and other platforms. Through these internet sources, al-Shabaab has been able to reach teens of Somali descent in the United Kingdom, the United States, and other countries to which their parents had immigrated. YouTube videos present al-Shabaab's point of view and compelling reasons why young people should come and fight against what they call oppression. According to the BBC, "al-Shabaab's well-produced video documentaries deliver the jihadi narrative in an appealing form to Somali audiences in the diaspora."

One producer of such videos is the al-Kataib Foundation. The foundation produces documentary-style films like *Mujahideen Moments 5* to depict a positive image of al-Shabaab engaging in charity work and appearing to have authority. Less appealingly, they also portray beheaded corpses of those they have killed, such as alleged spies. Films like this are designed to appeal to Somali who live abroad in the diaspora, inviting them back to their homeland to join radical groups like al-Shabaab.

Al-Shabaab also has its own radio network called Radio Andalus, which airs from private radio stations that the group has seized from other organizations. These stolen stations include even the BBC as well as HornAfrik, Holy Koran Radio, and the Global Broadcasting Corporation. By 2013, al-Shabaab had fifty journalists working for Radio Andalus. Material is presented mostly in Somali. However, some is presented in English with careful British or American accents, as well as in standard Arabic and Kiswahili (a language spoken in Tanzania and parts of Kenya). Over the past several years, the group has also used many different Twitter accounts, many of which have been closed down due to violating Twitter's policies.

Savvy in its marketing strategy and use of technology, al-Shabaab banned internet use on mobile phones in January 2014. They were aware of phones' tracking capabilities, which could be used to identify and trap al-Shabaab members. Prior to this, in 2013, al-Shabaab banned smart phones in areas they controlled, intimidating people who owned them. The group's members in Barawe also banned television, saying it violated Islamic principles. Residents were told to give up their TVs and satellite dishes to al-Shabaab officials.

## The Tipping Point

From the outside, it is hard to imagine reaching a point where joining a terrorist organization could seem like a logical choice. Yet for those who have grown up in situations where their lives are at risk daily, it is hard to know whom to trust. Many Somalian citizens feel that the government cannot be trusted to protect citizens' lives. In some cases, government actions have even caused harm to individuals. The Somali National Army (SNA) has, in the past, recruited children and teens to its own ranks. African Union troops, Ethiopian troops, the United States military, and the SNA have sometimes taken actions that resulted in harm or death for civilians, even children. Those casualties have caused people to lose trust. When people are suspicious of their own government, they are more likely to be swayed by rebels who promise a better future.

According to the UN Development Program, many factors can put people at risk of joining violent extremist groups. These factors include poverty and lack of education, but "the tipping point—that moment when a person decides to join the group—appears to be when an at-risk individual experienced a government arrest or killing of a family member or friend." A 2017 United Nations study found that for "a majority of cases, state [government] action appears to be the primary factor finally pushing individuals into violent extremism in Africa."

Therefore, the UN Development Program cautions that the way in which government behaves to counter terrorism is crucial. They urge, "more oversight of the state security sector in terms of human rights compliance, accountability, rule of law, and civilian participation is imperative." Until corruption is eliminated and human rights are supported, teens will continue to distrust the Somali government, making them vulnerable to recruitment.

## Leaving al-Shabaab and Rehabilitation Efforts

Once a young person has joined al-Shabaab, whether by force or by choice, leaving is hard to do. Often, the teen has nowhere to turn and no other prospects. These teens are typically young and vulnerable and lack resources. For some, al-Shabaab may come to feel like a type of family or kinship group. Therefore, loyalty to that group may keep them involved even if they doubt the mission or the methods.

UNICEF and the Somali government have worked together to try to remove child soldiers from danger and reintegrate them into their families. They provide psychosocial counseling, education, and other services. There is no doubt that future initiatives will need to include further attention to treating post-traumatic stress and other mental health issues in these populations that have been traumatized by violence.

One program working to provide viable alternate employment options for youth is the UNDP's Youth for Change Joint Initiative. The initiative focuses not only on fulfilling short-term needs for young people, but full rehabilitation and reintegration. These services help youth re-enter the educational system, become involved again in their communities in a productive way, and find job opportunities. The program works with youth who wish to leave piracy or radical groups in order to live a normal life.

## Abdikarim Ibrahim's Story

Abdikarim Ibrahim, age twenty-one, described his own previous desperate economic situation to staff at UNDP

# THE DOWNSIDES AND UPSIDES OF SOCIAL MEDIA

Most recruitment within Somalia still takes place face-to-face. Yet it is worth mentioning that al-Shabaab has become very savvy at using the internet and social media to reach Somali teens and youth outside their own country. Al-Shabaab recruits them to return to their homeland and fight for their heritage. This practice alarmed United States citizens in 2009, when nine Somali American men were recruited by al-Shabaab from Minneapolis, Minnesota. Minnesota has one of the largest Somali populations outside the country of Somalia. For the most part, this

Abdifatah Yusuf Isse was among a small group of teens who went missing from their hometown in Minnesota in 2009 and were later found to be plotting to join al-Shabaab. Isse served jail time and was later removed from the United States.

immigrant group has brought many positive things with them—spoken word poetry, delicious cultural foods, and dedication to academics. But in 2009, this small number of young Somali men in Minneapolis became radicalized and disappeared from the United States. The majority have died or have been arrested.

Somalia: "I grew up as an orphan in Bossaso. Being an orphan meant that you were doomed from the start. You had no one to stand up for you or take care of you. I had to do whatever I could to survive." Some development groups have taken a strategic stance to reduce the risks for young people. Abdikarim says,

> *This program changed my life, not because it provided me with money but because it changed the way I think about myself. I am not some helpless person who things just happen to. I matter and have control over my life. I am not a voiceless orphan—I am a contributing member of society.*

Now he works for a solar electricity company in Somalia's Bari region.

On October 15, 2017, part of Mogadishu was devastated by a truck bomb that is believed to have been set by al-Shabaab. More than four hundred people died in the explosion.

# CHAPTER FOUR

# THE CASUALTIES OF WAR AND TERROR

**A**lthough the Somali national government has regained control of much of the country, al-Shabaab continues to inflict suffering on people within Somalia with its frequent terror attacks. One of the deadliest attacks occurred on October 14, 2017. That day, a truck bomb blew up in the capital city of Mogadishu, killing at least 414 people and injuring hundreds more. Because of inadequate medical infrastructure within Somalia, more than fifty victims were transported to Turkey for treatment. Some remained there for more than a month. The *Guardian* reported that among those who died was medical student Maryam Abdullahi Gedi, age twenty-four, who was about to graduate from Banadir University. Her father had flown from the United Kingdom to see her graduate as a medical doctor but ended up attending her funeral instead. Her mother, Hinda Yusuf, said,

> *I lost the dearest one in my life. They killed my whole hope. I do not know why they killed my daughter … I ask al-Shabaab, "Why are you doing this bad on us?" God help us. My daughter was an extraordinary girl. She was a respectful student. She never confronted anyone in the family. All our neighbors loved her. We called her the "lovely one" due to her good character. I raised her in hardship. After leaving secondary school, she joined the university and it was her ambition to become a doctor.*

A day after the bombing, thousands of Somalis gathered to protest against al-Shabaab. (The terrorist group did not accept responsibility for the bombing but is widely believed to have planned it based on evidence.) The protesters wore red headbands and marched through the city of Mogadishu. Halima Abdullahi, who lost six relatives in terrorist attacks, told the *Guardian*, "We are demonstrating against the terrorists that massacred our people." Additional Somalis marched in other towns included Dusamareb in central Somalia.

Somali families rest as they travel from their drought-stricken homes in the Lower Shabelle to Mogadishu, where they will live in temporary shelters.

A driver of one of the trucks that detonated said that two months before the truck bombing, his hometown was raided by local troops and US forces. The operation had gone badly, killing ten civilians, three of them children. The driver said he had once been part of the Islamic Courts Union (ICU). Then, he had gone over to the Somali military in 2010 but had shifted to al-Shabaab around 2015. Some people blame the increased US military involvement, along with the increased number of civilian casualties, for strengthening support for al-Shabaab.

Another attack soon followed, this time acknowledged by al-Shabaab. On October 29, 2017, five members of al-Shabaab disguised in National Intelligence and Security Agency (NISA) uniforms took over a hotel frequented by government officials and killed at least twenty-three people. It was only two weeks after the truck bombing in Mogadishu.

# Ongoing Attacks in the Lower Shabelle Region

Outside of Mogadishu, in rural areas, attacks are more frequent, and al-Shabaab still wields powerful influence over people's lives. Southern parts of Somalia are still largely under al-Shabaab control or in the midst of violent clashes between different clans. Some clans ally with al-Shabaab or the national government, and some switch sides. This creates a volatile situation for civilians living there.

Earlier in 2017, from May to June, al-Shabaab burned several homes in the Lower Shabelle region of Somalia. Human Rights Watch used eyewitness accounts and satellite imagery to confirm numerous attacks, which caused fifteen thousand people to flee the area for safety. Civilians have been hit hard in the Lower Shabelle, where clan militias, federal government forces, al-Shabaab, and African Union forces violently clash on a frequent basis. One witness called "Abdi" (a nickname to protect his identity) told Human Rights Watch that "al-Shabaab accused us of joining the government. Some of our elders have talked to al-Shabaab and told them that those without guns should be spared. Initially they used to tax us, take livestock and money, but now they are burning our homes."

The United Nations reported that al-Shabaab also kidnapped seventy people from this area during two days in May and stole hundreds of livestock. Because of the ongoing drought, the theft of livestock can be deadly. (Livestock provide a much-needed source of milk and money.) The UN also found that about a hundred houses were burned and counted 15,240 people who were displaced between May 21 and May 24—just three days' time. These actions can be considered war crimes because they violate the international rules of war. The illegal actions include removing or abducting civilians without legitimate safety reasons, and pillaging, which means stealing private property for nonmilitary reasons.

## Day-to-Day Impacts

The effects of al-Shabaab's actions affect Somali lives on every level—ranging from restrictions in everyday activities like playing sports or choosing clothing all the way to the highest levels of societal organization. This includes having a functioning government to provide essentials like roads, schools, rule of law, and a fair and equitable justice system. Al-Shabaab cannot be entirely blamed for the absence of adequate educational, health, and legal systems. These structures were largely destroyed by civil war well before al-Shabaab rose to power. However, it is possible to point out specific ways in which al-Shabaab has worsened the situations and sometimes prevented assistance from reaching people who would have benefited from it.

## Devastated Infrastructure

Within Somalia, infrastructure is severely lacking. Under the Barre regime, modern advances in telecommunications and roads brought opportunities for the Somali people. But the combination of civil war since 1991 and terrorist activities since the early 2000s destroyed much of that. For example, for twenty-seven years, no flights were able to land in the country after dark because of the danger. In 2017, the first after-dark flight landed in Mogadishu, which was great cause for celebration. Still, only one airplane is registered in the country.

Al-Shabaab, in its clashes with both the national military and various clan militias, has badly damaged and blocked access to roads that connect small towns and villages to larger cities.

## Minimal Access to the World Wide Web and other Technologies

Slightly less than 2 percent of Somalia's population had access to the internet on a regular basis in 2017. Nationwide, the entire internet was shut down for weeks in the summer of 2017 due to a damaged undersea cable.

While al-Shabaab isn't entirely to blame for the weak telecommunication infrastructure, it certainly has contributed to the problem. As previously mentioned, al-Shabaab banned smartphones in 2013 because they feared that phones could be used by spies or informants trying to track their movements. The Internet Freedom Project reports that al-Shabaab terrorists frequently attack satellite towers. In 2014, al-Shabaab was powerful enough to threaten and demand that Somali telecom companies shut down 3G mobile internet service. The companies actually complied out of fear.

The first underground fiber-optic cables came to Mogadishu later in 2014, bringing high-speed connections and reducing the possibility of damage from attacks. Yet the service is very expensive at about $50 per month. For a country where most people live on a dollar per day, internet service is completely out of reach.

# The Toll on Physical Health

People in Somalia have very limited access to the basic necessities like clean water, sanitation, and adequate food. According to the World Health Organization, in 2012, males born in Somalia had a 45 percent chance of dying before they reached age fifteen, and females had a 40 percent chance of dying before the age of fifteen. The UN Refugee Agency reported in September 2017 that due to drought and violence, there were 3.2 million people in Somalia facing severe food insecurity. The report clearly shows the negative role that al-Shabaab plays as it disrupts the ability of aid workers to help needy people.

# The Toll on Mental and Emotional Health

The UNHCR has conducted extensive research about the mental health issues specific to Somali refugees, returnees, and those of Somali descent who have settled permanently in other countries. The extent of mental health issues is difficult for experts to determine. This is because of the difficulty of collecting data in unstable regions combined with the significant cultural and language differences in describing states of distress. For example, some symptoms that Westerners might attribute to mental illness or biological causes, in Somalia, are considered to be the result of God's will, or of supernatural forces called jinn (a kind of possession recognized in Islam), or *sar* (in pre-Islamic beliefs thought to be indigenous to northeastern Somalia).

Sometimes the suffering is believed to be caused by social and economic difficulties, loss of a job or a loved one, or traumatic events associated with war. In these cases, family members may try to help the person by simply letting them rest or, if that fails, by seeking professional treatment.

It is clear among those who work with Somali survivors of torture and trauma that these victims suffer lasting effects. The Center for Victims of Torture (CVT) notes complaints of headaches, dizziness, unexplained bodily pains, poor memory, and poor concentration. Survivors describe feelings of hopelessness, irritability, helplessness, and loneliness. Among tortured women, especially those who have survived sexual or gender-based violence, symptoms included chronic lower abdominal pain and irregular menses. Sometimes survivors of torture become involved in risky behaviors or abuse drugs, such as khat, a kind of drug that is chewed in East Africa, and alcohol.

The Somali culture includes a significant degree of stigma with regard to mental health and seeking treatment. However, the language includes several rich ways of expressing the pain of what other cultures would describe as anxiety, depression, post-traumatic stress and other disorders. The UN Refugee Agency reports on some of the Somali terms used to describe negative emotional states: *murug* (sorrow or sadness), *qlbi-jab* (broken heart), *niyad-jab* (broken mind or will), or *welwel* (too much worry). Somalis think of these conditions as the result of outside events rather than an internal state. They do not typically seek help from the health sector for these feelings. Instead, they usually turn to extended family or clan members for support. People with *waali* (the Somali term of severe mental disorders, or "madness"), however, are not well accepted. They may be subjected to human rights abuses such as many months of being chained up, being unallowed to marry or hold a job, and isolation.

Terrorist activities cause disruption to communities and can make symptoms worse for individuals predisposed to symptoms of anxiety, depression, and other illnesses. Experiencing torture, witnessing violence and killings, and the inability to accomplish life goals are ways in which al-Shabaab's activities, in particular, affect mental health among Somalis. Both those living within the country and those who are forced to flee for safety experience ill effects. Furthermore, terrorist activities disrupt the social structures that would normally serve as sources of support for people seeking resources beyond themselves.

# The Toll on Education

While al-Shabaab is not solely to blame for Somalia's low rates of education and low literacy, the group's restrictions and actions have contributed to worsening the problem. First, there is the short history of formal education within the country. Apart from religious education consisting of studying the Quran, formal education has been a relatively recent development. For as long as living memory, the Somali language has traditionally existed in oral form only. It was only in 1972, under Barre's rule, that a written form was created using Latin letters. Then publicly funded schools began teaching literacy. But with the fall of Barre in 1991, the education system was, for the most part, dismantled. As of 2016, the World Health Organization found that when Somali women were asked to read a simple sentence about everyday life, only about 25 percent were able to do so. The lack of literacy leaves people vulnerable to misinformation and false narratives and prevents them from communicating with the outside world. Their voices cannot easily be heard. New economic opportunities are also harder to come by.

A young Somali woman named Nawa told her story to refugee workers with the UN Refugee Agency. By age sixteen, she had never been given the opportunity to attend any kind of school. As a refugee, and especially as a female, she didn't have access to classrooms or educational materials. She'd never been taught how to read. After arriving in a different refugee center in Malaysia, she was given her first backpack filled with school supplies and enrolled in a school for refugees. She recalls,

> I spent sixteen years not having access to education and wanting to learn so badly. When I first got my backpack to start Fugee School, I would literally put it on and stare at the mirror just imagining myself as a student. I started in fifth grade with classmates who were ten years old or younger. They made fun of me, but I tried to ignore it.

She failed her first classes because of her very limited grasp of English and her illiteracy in Somali. But with very hard work, she accomplished a lot. She says, "What drives me is that I'm the only person in my family to have access to education and to have gotten this far. I also want to be an example to other women who are afraid to achieve the things they want."

In Somalia, historically, women often marry during their teenage years. This has meant the end of any opportunity for

Small children in a refugee camp in Hargeisa, Somalia, in 2010

formal education. Therefore, female Somali students tend to prize education when they can get it and work very hard. Nawa, for example, mastered twelve years of schooling in just four years. By age twenty, Nawa received a scholarship to study at a university in Malaysia. According to the UN Refugee Agency, only 1 per cent of refugees go to college or university—a much lower figure than the general population. Nawa says, "Refugees have been through war and been forced to move so much, so our education is not stable. We have to do extra work and work harder than the locals."

Aid groups are finding ways to integrate new mobile technologies, however, to bring online-based education to Somali refugees. One example is the Instant Network Schools. The initiative is a collaboration between the UN Refugee Agency (UNHCR) and the Vodafone Foundation, which provides kits to selected schools and community centers in refugee camps. The UNHCR reports that each kit includes "computer tablets, solar-powered batteries, a satellite or mobile network, and a suite of content and online learning material. Teachers receive IT support and ongoing training."

Vodafone and UNHCR worked together to first try this model in Dadaab, Kenya, in 2014. There, hundreds of thousands of refugees have been living for many years without adequate access to quality education. Worldwide, about half of all twenty-one million refugees are children. Just 50 percent of them attend primary school, while only 22 percent are in secondary school. Refugee schools are usually overcrowded and lack necessary resources. But integrating Information Communication and Technology (ICT) has increased motivation for both students and teachers and allows learners to see the world beyond their refugee camp—sometimes for the first time.

## Ongoing Violence and Refugees

Although more than one hundred thousand Somali refugees have voluntarily returned home since 2014, attacks by al-Shabaab are a reminder that Somalia is not yet as safe as it

UNICEF operates this school for refugee children and IDP on the outskirts of Hargeisa, Somalia.

should be. Such violent attacks also hamper the efforts to resettle more returnees in the future.

## The State of Refugees and Internally Displaced Persons

One of the most noticeable impacts of terrorism in not only Somalia, but in its neighboring countries, is the high number of internally displaced people (IDP) and refugees. Somalis love their homeland, so they choose to flee only as an absolute last resort. Yet well over one million Somalis are IDP, meaning that while they remain within their country's borders, they have no permanent housing. In October 2017, the UNHCR reported that they were responsible for looking after more than 1.6 million IDP within Somalia.

These people live in camps or tent cities, or sometimes with kind strangers, relying on humanitarian aid whenever it is available. This is a very uncertain way to survive.

Desperation sometimes drives displaced persons to leave their homeland, seeking refugee status in neighboring Kenya, Ethiopia, or Djibouti, or in another African nation. In addition to the 1.7 million IDP, another estimated one million Somalis are living outside their nation's borders because violence caused them to flee for their lives.

The largest number of Somali refugees live in Kenya, Ethiopia, and Djibouti. For over two decades, such refugees have lived in temporary camps like the five near Dadaab in Kenya. These camps house more than two hundred thousand refugees, most of who are from Somalia. Because the crisis has been going on for so long, however, a second generation of Somalis is being born as refugees.

Some refugees make the risky journey over the Mediterranean Sea, hoping to find kindness on the other side. Yemen, for instance, has hosted Somali refugees for many years. Other Somalis are able to make their way into Saudi Arabia or to Europe. Still others cross over to North America and find new homes in the United States or Canada. Virtually every nation has been affected in recent years by the mass amounts of immigrants coming from Somalia. Only two other countries produce greater numbers of refugees: Syria and Afghanistan.

Outside of the continent of Africa, the nations that host the most Somali refugees are the United States, the United Kingdom, and Canada. Minnesota, in the United States, has a sizeable Somali population estimated at about 150,000, although exact numbers are not available.

According to the Voice of America news network, those who choose to flee are often victims of human trafficking or smuggling. Some suffer rape and abuse while on boats from Somalia en route to Yemen and elsewhere. In August 2017, smugglers threw refugees into the ocean at gunpoint before reaching the shore of Yemen. Many drowned and washed up on the beach where they were buried in shallow graves. Reporters were shocked to discover that most of these smuggled Somalis and Ethiopians were just sixteen or seventeen years old and had left home because they were orphaned or their families had been imprisoned for protesting.

Despite the horrible traveling conditions, survivors said it was better to die traveling than to remain where they were at home. This is because they believe that those who survive have a chance of building a better life in Saudi Arabia or elsewhere. They hope to find jobs and send money to their extended families in the future. If they remain in Somalia or Ethiopia, they are at high risk of death from starvation or from violence. This violence is at the hands of either terrorists or their own governments, which crack down on protesters or mistreat people from minority groups.

## Samia Yusuf Omar's Story

The UN Refugee Agency website published the story of Somali teenager Samia Yusuf Omar. Omar competed as a sprinter in the 2008 Beijing Olympics and was determined to compete again at the 2012 London Games. At seventeen years of age, Omar represented her country and ran in the 200-meter sprint. Although she came in last, the crowd roared to see her inspiring finish. She dreamed of doing better in the 2012 Olympics. But training as a runner in Somalia is full of obstacles. Because her nation was consumed with fighting between government forces, Islamist rebels such as al-Shabaab, and clan warlords, there were no available

Seventeen-year-old Samia Yusuf Omar competed for Somalia in the 2008 Olympics in Beijing, China.

sports facilities because they were being used as barracks. Furthermore, Omar was threatened by al-Shabaab. These threats were both because the national Olympic team was seen as connected to the government (which al-Shabaab rejected) and because wearing shorts as a woman was perceived as immodest.

Desperate to continue training, in 2010, Omar decided to make her way to Ethiopia where sports facilities existed. Unfortunately, she wasn't able to renew her visa there. Next, she decided to try to migrate to Europe. She would have to first pass through Sudan, the Sahara Desert, and Libya. At one point during her journey, she was kidnapped and held for ransom. Somehow she escaped, made it to the coast, and got into a boat headed across the Mediterranean Sea. Tragically, like so many ill-fated refugees, she died along the way.

## The Perils of Crossing the Mediterranean

When migrants finally board the boats to set sail, often the boats are packed with far more people than they should carry. For example, on September 21, 2016, a boat designed to hold 40 people was crossing the Mediterranean packed with more than 350 refugees and migrants. These people came from Syria, Eritrea, Sudan, Somalia, and elsewhere. The boat sank off the coast of Egypt, drowning 203 of its passengers. Afterward, more than 56 people were charged with various

# US INVOLVEMENT IN SOMALIA: ON THE GROUND AND BY LAW

The United States became involved in Somalia again in 2017 to a degree not seen since the early 1990s. Since 1993, when the incident known as "Black Hawk Down" resulted in the deaths of US soldiers, Americans have avoided overt military action in Somalia. (However, as members of the United Nations, they were involved in decision-making about sending UN troops.) Under President Obama, the United States increased pressure on al-Shabaab through military drone strikes, which are unmanned craft that drop bombs on targets. Under President Trump, the United States has increased its military interventions. This move has been controversial in Somalia because of the risk of increased civilian deaths. The United States has completed over thirty drone strikes in 2017. The increased military involvement came not as a result of a specific terrorism incident, but as the result of a pledge that Trump made during his campaign to fight "radical Islamist terrorism."

In addition, in 2017, Somalia was included in a list of countries from which people were banned from traveling to the United States. The first few versions of a travel ban, which was initiated shortly after President Trump took office in January

2017, were blocked in US federal courts multiple times because they discriminated against people based on their nationality and/or religion. These courts found that the ban violated the US Constitution. All of the countries included in the first two versions of the travel ban were Muslim-majority countries: Iran, Syria, Libya, Sudan, Somalia, and Yemen. The third version of the ban included eight countries: Chad, Iran, Libya, North Korea, Syria, Venezuela, Somalia, and Yemen. In December 2017, the United States Supreme Court allowed Trump's third version of the travel ban to go into effect. This means that citizens from these eight countries are no longer allowed to emigrate permanently to the US. Notably, Somalis in particular may no longer emigrate but may be allowed to visit after being subjected to extra screening. Understandably, this comes as a blow to Somali Americans wishing to stay connected or to reunite with extended family.

This boat near Aden, Yemen, is crowded with refugees traveling from Somalia, hoping to start a new life in a safer country.

crimes including "manslaughter, smuggling, fraud, and using boats for unlicensed purposes," the UNHDR reports.

Despite the danger, in 2017, about 100,000 people, including Somalis and refugees from other African countries, have crossed the Mediterranean from Libya. In Libya, before crossing, many of them faced being kidnapped, beaten, starved, and being sold to smugglers.

The UN Refugee Agency is aware of at least 8,500 migrants, including many children and teenagers, who have died on the Mediterranean between September 2015 and August 2017. Yet despite the deadly danger, young people motivated by hope and fear continue to persist in immigrating.

# REFUGEE SUCCESS STORIES

Refugee populations experience vastly different futures depending on where they are living. Some live in tent cities like those in Dadaab, Kenya. Others find comfortable new lives in safety, such as those who settle in Wisconsin or Minnesota. When developed countries like Saudi Arabia, the United Kingdom, Sweden, and the United States are able to absorb refugees, life can return to a kind of normalcy.

A remarkable refugee story is that of Mohamed Abdullahi Mohamed, commonly known by the nickname Farmajo. He lived in Buffalo, New York, as a Somali refugee for many years. Then he returned home to his country in 2017 to serve as president!

In the United States, some Somali American women are working to provide better representation of women in government. A key example is Somali American Ilhan Omar, who was recently elected to the Minnesota state house of representatives.

Finally, an interesting example of refugee entrepreneurship is the story of Somali refugee women living in Ethiopia who have banded together to form a milk-selling cooperative. They collect the milk from camels and cows, then pasteurize it to make it safe for consumption. Members divide up the money to reinvest in the business as well as to provide for themselves and for each other.

These Somali men, convicted of piracy or suspected of having ties to al-Shabaab, are imprisoned in Garowe, Puntland. This prison works to rehabilitate former pirates and soldiers so they can resume a more normal life when they return to their communities.

# CHAPTER FIVE

# SOLVING TERROR

An article on the UNICEF website features stories about what happens to former al-Shabaab members after they are recruited to fight—and are then caught. One seventeen-year-old boy called Aden (his name was changed to protect his safety) shared his story about being abducted the previous year from a coastal town in Puntland. His uncle pretended to take Aden out to dinner one day in 2016, but actually took him to an al-Shabaab military base. He and the other teen boys were taught how to use guns, then had to accompany al-Shabaab fighters on a raid in northeast Somalia. After a night of fighting, Aden, along with sixty-five other boys under the age of eighteen, was captured by Somali security forces. After this, authorities transferred boys younger than fifteen to a UNICEF Center in Mogadishu, but Aden and the other boys fifteen and older were sentenced to ten to twenty years' imprisonment.

Fortunately for Aden, the UN and the international community intervened to convince the authorities to send the teens to a rehabilitation center in Garowe instead of to prison. Aden says, "I was so scared when I was taken to prison. Now I am at the center and I get food, shelter and an education and I also get to speak to my mother and father every day." Aden and other former child soldiers receive psychosocial support to help them cope with what they have been through. Aden says, "I am safe here and I am learning so much. But when I get home, I am going to study hard and then I want to become a businessman and create opportunities for young people."

# The Big Task of Peacebuilding

Aden's story is just one example of why solving terrorism is not an easy task. Peacebuilding takes time, patience, and willingness to learn from mistakes made in the past. Many experts have weighed in on what they believe are the best options for disrupting al-Shabaab. Hindsight is more accurate than trying to predict outcomes, so analysts have looked carefully at which interventions have worked in the past and which have not. Learning from the past can help inform better policies and interventions for the future.

Universities, research institutes, the US Department of Defense, the nonpartisan Center for Foreign Policy, the United Nations, and many other expert analysts have studied what kinds of efforts have been tried thus far and what the consequences were. Both military and nonmilitary interventions have been studied. While there are divergent opinions on what should be done next, most sources agree on what has not worked well.

The most important point of agreement is that the violence cannot be stopped by adding more violence and

Al-Shabaab attacked the Westgate shopping mall in Nairobi, Kenya, in September of 2013. This image shows the damage done to a parking deck. This was the first major attack by al-Shabaab outside Somalia's borders.

weapons. It has become clear that taking excessively punitive or harsh approaches toward members of terrorist groups can often have the opposite effect from what is desired. Instead of stopping the groups, military intervention sometimes has made people more sympathetic to the terrorists. This is because the terrorists' storyline is that the government and foreign military groups cannot be trusted. When civilians are accidentally killed by drone strikes or missed targets, or when child soldiers are given lengthy prison sentences, al-Shabaab uses that as evidence that the counterterrorism forces are the "bad guys." Therefore, national and international actors must observe the rule of law, respect basic human rights, and demonstrate a commitment to justice by providing fair trials, adequate evidence, and due process under the law before executing those accused of terrorist activities. Only then will civilians trust the government more than the terrorists and extremists.

## The Challenges of Containing Terrorism

One problem that has been observed is that even when military forces have defeated al-Shabaab and driven them out of power in certain regions, the mindsets of its members may not have changed. These same fighters then find new ways to keep inflicting terror on others—whether by moving outside the country or joining a different organization. For example, as al-Shabaab was being driven out of Mogadishu in Somalia, they began to organize attacks in neighboring Kenya. These included mass killings at the Westgate shopping mall and Garissa University. Some soldiers have shifted loyalty from al-Shabaab to local clan militias or Somali national forces. In 2012, al-Shabaab allied with al-Qaeda. Al-Qaeda focuses not only on Somalia but on threatening and attacking countries around the globe.

Taking out individual fighters may not work, either, since that fighter's family and friends may see the loss of their loved one as an incentive to join al-Shabaab or another antigovernment force in revenge.

## Non-Military Solutions

According to author Abdisaid Musse Ali-Koor, who has studied Islamist extremism in East Africa, there are many nonmilitary actions that can help reduce its spread. First, it is important to emphasize the long history of tolerance in the region. Well before the destabilizing messages of extremism came to the region, East Africans tolerated many different practices and beliefs associated with Islam. Ali-Koor cautions, however, that "blanket criminalization of conservative Islamic groups should be avoided as this will likely spur more support for violent movements. Rather, a policy of tolerance with a clear prohibition against violence and divisiveness should be pursued."

According to Ali-Koor, in the past, "religious communities in [East Africa], whether Muslim or non-Muslim, have historically tended to coexist peacefully and overlook any differences in theology or religious practice," but this has changed since the 1990s and 2000s. He blames the growing influence of Salafist ideology, which is strict and rigid compared to the Sufi-influenced type of Islam historically prevalent in Somalia and has "changed their relationship with other Muslims, with other faiths, and with the state." One of the reasons for this is the increasing numbers of East Africans studying in conservative Muslim countries that practice less tolerance. As counterterrorist policies in Western countries limit opportunities for Africans to study in Europe and the United States, these students go instead to Saudi Arabia, United Arab Emirates, Turkey, and elsewhere in the Middle East, where they are taught more fundamentalist versions of Islam.

A second reason for changing interpretations of Islam is the access to media in the Arab world, such as Arab satellite TV stations, which convey "more conservative interpretations of Islam regarding dress, the role of women, and differentiated relationships between Muslims and non-Muslims." Wahhabism, an extremely conservative interpretation of the Quran, forbids some parts of modern education and limits basic human rights, particularly for women.

In addition, Ali-Koor says it will be important to invest in citizens so that they have better chances economically and institutionally. This means that programs should help provide equal opportunity for all in education. Whether rural or urban, and regardless of income, everyone should have access to an education. Improving property rights within Eastern Africa would also help people to feel that the government is protecting them and their interests.

Third, all recognized governments must abide by the rule of law, due process under the law, and observe human rights—even when prosecuting those accused of terrorist actions. Quick, unfair trials without good evidence only do more harm, since governments that appear vindictive to al-Shabaab members may cause people to feel sorry for the terrorists. This is especially true when child soldiers are sentenced to death or long periods of imprisonment. Ali-Koor urges that "Extrajudicial police action must also stop immediately." The government should instead support clear, fair investigations by independent experts to evaluate all claims about what al-Shabaab has done. Then, all the findings need to be made public so that people will rebuild trust in their own government.

Most importantly, rather than focusing on the crimes of particular individuals, counterterrorism efforts must "delegitimize the ideology of violent extremism itself." This means that rather than focusing on punishing terrorists for what they have done, society and government must uphold a higher standard for all human rights—even the rights of those who have done wrong. They must break down the misguided narrative that violence is ever a viable solution to conflict.

## Abdi's and Ali's Stories

UNICEF interviewed seventeen-year-old Abdi, who was once an al-Shabaab fighter but is now training to be an electrician. He says, "I used to be brave—a lion—among the soldiers. I was at war, fighting against other groups." He explains his early impression of al-Shabaab. "At the beginning, we thought these people were good. Their ideology was based on religion. But then we realized that their ideology was misinterpretations of Islam. They were doing nothing by harming the communities we belong to. So I left." Once he returned home, his family was happy, but he didn't have a job or any productive way to spend his time. Then he got connected with a vocational training program for former child soldiers. He was able to choose between carpentry, plumbing, electrical, or tailoring. Abdi says, "I envision myself finishing this course and then finding a good job as a professional electrician."

UNICEF estimates that as many as six thousand children and teens may still be within the ranks of various armed groups in the southern and central regions of Somalia. Vocational training programs are an important component of helping child soldiers find new, productive skills that will help them return to making meaningful contributions in their society. Another teen and former soldier, Ali, told UNICEF staff in 2016, "It is very stressful to be with those groups. For those who are thinking of joining, I would ask them to think again. It will not give you a good life. Only empowering ourselves through education can give us a good life. Never join the groups. It will only lead you to death."

# The Role of Women and Youth in Fighting Terrorism

## Women as Peacemakers

Other experts have added that more attention should be given to the vital role that women and youth can play in combating terrorism and promoting development. For instance, American foreign policy experts Jamille Bigio and Rachel Vogelstein advocate for more active participation by women in counterterrorism and peacemaking activities. The Council on Foreign Relations has performed research about women's involvement in peace negotiations and how their participation in conflict prevention and resolution is helpful to US interests. They have found that when women are involved, the resulting agreements are less likely to fail and are more likely to last long-term. In addition, these experts notice that "higher levels of gender equality are associated with a lower propensity for conflict, both between and within states."

Yet women have often been overlooked and underrepresented in peace talks. For example, between 1992 and 2011, "women represented fewer than 4 percent" of those who signed peace agreements. Therefore, these experts urge that more effort should be made to include women in peace agreements and conflict-prevention strategies in order to have better, more successful outcomes.

At age nineteen, Iman Elman joined the Somali National Army because she had witnessed terrible violence and wanted to take action against it. Her father, a peace activist, had been killed by those who opposed his activism. As of 2017, she is the highest-ranking woman in the Somali National Army, at age twenty-four. She has presented TED talks and given other speeches about the role women can play in combatting terrorism. Although some people find it ironic that Iman Elman's father was a peace activist and she is in the military, Elman sees her role as working toward the same goal of long-term stability, security, and peace in her home country.

## Youth as Peacemakers

Youth are another important demographic to consider in counterterrorism strategies. The United Nations has been working to improve the representation that young people have in their governments and the public sector. One initiative called the Global Youth Call came up with a list of actions to improve conditions for teens. It included several categories on which governments and aid organizations should focus in order to improve the lives of young people. These include education, employment and entrepreneurship, health, peace and personal security, and governance and participation.

The document specifies that when it comes to decision-making, young people should be more included at local, national, regional, and global levels. Marginalized youth need to have the right to information, association, and freedom of speech and opinion. Youth-led movements can be strengthened and given better access to institutions that make

# SOUTH CENTRAL SOMALI YOUTH UMBRELLA

In 2009, a group of Somali youth living in Mogadishu formed a nonprofit organization called South Central Somali Youth Umbrella (SOCSOYU) with the goal of rehabilitating the lives of their peers through activities such as participating in the arts, sports, and peaceful dialogue. They wanted to give Somali youth the opportunity to voice their concerns about their lives and their country. Their objectives are to improve the quality of education, human rights, rural water quality, peacebuilding, and daily life. One of their campaigns, called "Think of Your Family," focuses on the stories of families whose loved one has joined an extremist group. This storytelling campaign is designed to help young people understand the consequences of their actions and the impact of their choices on the families they leave behind.

A second campaign by SOCSOYU is called "Open Talk" (or *madal furan*, in Somali), which celebrates the young people who are working at the grassroots level to bring better peace and security to their city of Mogadishu. It is designed to help young people understand how they can contribute to peace and security in their own neighborhoods. More information about this group is available on Twitter under the hashtag #MadalFuran, with posts in both Somali and in English.

decisions that affect them. Finally, youth should be involved in holding their leadership and governments accountable for their actions.

Within Somalia, several initiatives have been set up with the goal of helping young people. For starters, the country has a Ministry of Youth and Sports. The ministry was created in 2007 to help youth become more involved in the democratic process. In October 2014, the federal government of Somalia asked the United Nations Population Fund and UN-Habitat, the UN's Human Settlements Programme, to develop a National Youth Policy. Leaders recognized the need for youth to have the chance to work on development goals and participate in decision-making.

Government and aid groups are also spending more time and resources on developing programs targeting the rehabilitation of youth who have either joined terrorist organizations and left, or who are vulnerable to being recruited.

An example of one such intervention is in Puntland, where viable economic alternatives to piracy are cropping up. Additional youth rehabilitation programs are being developed in Somalia, Somaliland, and Puntland. UNICEF has partnered with many other organizations to build rehabilitation programs and vocational training like the ones in which Abdi and Ali participated after leaving al-Shabaab.

# Reducing the Risks

The more society works toward promoting human rights where all individuals are respected and protected, with access to opportunity, education, and meaningful work, the less appeal terrorist organizations will have.

Somali Youth Ambassador Fatima Abdi Ali once wrote, "It may sound strange—but being a young person in Somalia today is a golden opportunity. It is the youth who have the chance to rebuild a country which suffered years of war—where every sector of life needs change makers, peace promoters, scientists, entrepreneurs and fresh young leaders are full of positive energy." More than any other age group, youths have the power to make the most change in Somalia's future. With the election of President Farmajo in February 2017, and the continuing weakening of al-Shabaab, the young people of Somalia have reason to be optimistic that change is indeed possible.

# LEVERAGING THE INTERNET

**S**ince the internet arrived in Somalia, many people are finding it a useful tool for improving security and opportunities within the country. They can check their phones for alerts before leaving home, for example, and avoid parts of the city where something dangerous is happening. They can connect with the broader world, too, and run businesses and nonprofit organizations. The individuals who are online have demonstrated how resourceful they can be. Voice of America published a story about several residents of Mogadishu who use the internet in a variety of meaningful ways.

Video blogger and photographer Mukhtar Nuur shares his work on Facebook, YouTube, and Twitter. Viewers will see young people enjoying a boat ride on a beautiful blue-skied day near Mogadishu's Lido Beach. Zahra Qorane shares pictures of her home city via social media, showing the positive aspects of Mogadishu, which are too often ignored in global media. Musician Khadar Keyow posts his performances on YouTube to reach a broader audience. Entrepreneur Sahar Abdikarim works in the tech industry, proving that women can run tech-related businesses just as men can. And Ayan Mohamed used a social media campaign to collect books and funds in order to open a public library, since most of Somalia's libraries have been closed since the start of the civil war in 1991.

# CHRONOLOGY

**1960**  Two Somaliland colonies (one Italian and one British) gain independence and join into one country called the United Republic of Somalia.

**1991**  President Mohamed Barre's military regime is overthrown, resulting in anarchy. The former British Somaliland declares itself independent and sets up its own government.

**1998**  The northern region of Puntland declares itself autonomous (but not independent).

**2005–2012**
Somali pirates pose problems for international trade.

**2010**  Al-Shabaab announces it will ally with al-Qaeda; the merger becomes official in 2012.

**2013**  The United States officially recognizes the Somali government in Mogadishu : Al-Shabaab attacks Westgate shopping complex in Nairobi, Kenya, killing more than thirty and injuring hundreds.

**2017**  The election of a new president, Mohamed Abdullahi Mohamed, marks a significant change : An al-Shabaab truck bomb kills more than 300 in Mogadishu, Somalia.

# GLOSSARY

**al-Qaeda** The terrorist organization responsible for the September 11 attacks. These attacks led the president of the United States, George W. Bush, to declare a "war on terror."

**hijab** A scarf or head-covering that is worn by some Muslim women to cover their hair for modesty. The term refers to many different styles.

**internally displaced person (IDP)** Someone who has fled from home due to violence but remains within his or her home country's borders.

**jilbab** Refers to any long or loose-fitting garment or coat that covers the body and is worn by some Muslim women.

**khat** A plant in East Africa chewed to produce a sense of euphoria.

**niqab** A controversial garment that covers the face except for the eyes, worn by a small number of conservative Muslim women, usually those belonging to the Salafist branch of Islam.

**nomad** Someone whose way of life consists of moving from place to place, often following seasonal patterns related to water and grazing lands.

**pastoralist** A person whose way of life relies on grazing animals such as cattle, camels, goats, and sheep.

**radicalization** A process in which someone's thinking patterns become increasingly narrow, rejecting other commonly accepted points of view.

**refugee** Someone who has fled his or her country due to life-threatening safety issues.

**returnee** Someone who has previously lived as a refugee or immigrant but has returned home to resettle.

**semiautonomous region** An area that has declared a separation from its country but which has not been officially recognized.

**terrorism** Criminal acts carried out with the purpose of inflicting a state of fear on the general population.

**violent extremism** Messages of intolerance—which may be religious, cultural, or social in nature—that inspire followers to take violent actions against those with different beliefs.

# FURTHER INFORMATION

## Books

Harding, Andrew. *The Mayor of Mogadishu: A Story of Chaos and Redemption in the Ruins of Somalia*. New York: St. Martin's Press, 2016.

Kleist, Reinhard. *An Olympic Dream: The Story of Samia Yusuf Omar*. London, UK: SelfMadeHero, 2016.

Okeowo, Alexis. *A Moonless, Starless Sky: Ordinary Women and Men Fighting Extremism in Africa*. New York: Hachette Books, 2017.

## Websites

**CIA World Factbook: Somalia**

https://www.cia.gov/library/publications/
the-world-factbook/geos/so.html

Explore statistics, maps, and the latest information about the country of Somalia.

**Human Rights Watch: Somalia**

https://www.hrw.org/africa/somalia

Learn more about the obstacles Somalis face due to war, terrorism, and human rights abuses.

**UNICEF: Somalia**

https://www.unicef.org/somalia/reallives_18557.html

Find a teen's firsthand account of youth working for change in Somalia, photo essays, and a link to UNICEF: Somalia's Instagram account on this site.

## Videos

**"Semblance of normality in Somalia's capital despite terror attacks"**

https://www.youtube.com/watch?v=iUWudOWiJZE

See footage of Mogadishu and hear more about the looming threat of al-Shabaab in this December 2017 report from CBS Evening News.

**"Somalia: The Forgotten Story"**

https://www.youtube.com/watch?v=-io_RfLBpgc

*Al Jazeera World* presents a detailed look at the history of Somalia that led from "stability to chaos."

# BIBLIOGRAPHY

"Al-Shabab Mukhtar Robow Defects to Government Side."
Al Jazeera, August 13, 2017. http://www.aljazeera.com/
news/2017/08/al-shabab-mukhtar-robow-defects-
government-side-170813141245475.html.

Ali-Koor, Abdisaid Musse. "Islamist Extremism in East
Africa." *Africa Security Brief No. 32*. Africa Center for
Strategic Studies, August 9, 2016. https://africacenter.
org/publication/islamist-extremism-east-africa/.

Bigio, Jamille, and Rachel Vogelstein. *How Women's
Participation in Conflict Prevention and Resolution
Advances U.S. Interests*. New York: Council on Foreign
Relations Press, 2016.

Cilliers, Jakkie. "Violent Islamist Extremism and Terror in
Africa." Institute for Security Studies, October 2015.
https://issafrica.s3.amazonaws.com/site/uploads/
Paper286-1.pdf.

Felter, Claire, Jonathan Masters, and Mohammed Aly
Sergie. "Al-Shabaab." Council on Foreign Relations,
March 2015. https://www.cfr.org/backgrounder/al-
shabab.

The Global Youth Call. "Prioritizing Youth in the Post-2015
Development Agenda." United Nations, June 3, 2014. http://
www.un.org/youthenvoy/wp-content/uploads/2014/09/
The-Global-Call-on-Youth_with-endorsements_3-
June-2014.pdf.

Hess, Amanda. "Warsan Shire, the Woman Who Gave
Poetry to Beyoncé's 'Lemonade.'" *New York Times*,
April 27, 2016. https://www.nytimes.com/2016/04/28/
arts/music/warsan-shire-who-gave-poetry-to-beyonces-
lemonade.html.

Karmi, Omar. "An Olympic Dream, Shattered." UNHCR,
April 11, 2016. http://www.unhcr.org/en-us/news/
stories/2016/4/573af4634/an-olympic-dream-shattered.html.

Kessels, Eelco, Tracey Dumer, and Matthew Schwartz. "Violent
Extremism and Instability in the Greater Horn of Africa: An
Examination of Drivers and Responses." Global Center on
Cooperative Security, April 2016. http://www.globalcenter.
org/publications/violent-extremism-and-instability-in-the-
greater-horn-of-africa/.

Nantulya, Paul. "A Review of Africa Center Research on
Terrorism and Countering Violent Extremism." Africa Center
for Strategic Studies, April 2, 2014. https://africacenter.
org/spotlight/africa-center-research-terrorism-countering-
violent-extremism/.

UNDP. *Journey to Extremism in Africa.* Regional Bureau
    for Africa, 2017. http://journey-to-extremism.undp.org/
    content/downloads/UNDP-JourneyToExtremism-report-
    2017-english.pdf.

_____. "Somalia." 2017. http://www.so.undp.org/
    content/somalia/en/home/countryinfo.html.

UN Refugee Agency (UNHCR). "Situation in the Horn of
    Africa." Retrieved December 1, 2017.  https://data2.
    unhcr.org/en/situations/horn.

Warner, Jason. "Sub-Saharan Africa's Three 'New' Islamic
    State Affiliates." Combating Terrorism Center Sentinel
    10.1 (2017): 28-32. https://ctc.usma.edu/v2/wp-content/
    uploads/2017/01/CTC- Sentinel_Vol9Iss1119.pdf.

World Health Organization. "Somalia." Retrieved December
    1, 2017.  www.who.int/countries/som/en/.

# INDEX

Page numbers in **boldface**
are illustrations

# ABOUT THE AUTHOR

**Anna Maria Johnson** teaches courses in writing, research, and the humanities at James Madison University. She also writes and edits books and essays for a variety of audiences, ranging from elementary school to the graduate school level. Anna Maria lives with her husband and their two teenage daughters near Harrisonburg, Virginia, a designated refugee resettlement city.